# I Am a Dolphin
## The Life of a Bottlenose Dolphin

by Darlene R. Stille  illustrated by Todd Ouren

Special thanks to our advisers for their expertise:

Susan H. Shane, Ph.D., Biology
University of California at Santa Cruz

Susan Kesselring, M.A., Literacy Educator
Rosemount-Apple Valley-Eagan (Minnesota) School District

## I Live in the Ocean

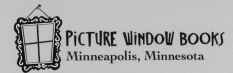

PICTURE WINDOW BOOKS
Minneapolis, Minnesota

Managing Editors: Bob Temple, Catherine Neitge
Creative Director: Terri Foley
Editors: Nadia Higgins, Patricia Stockland
Editorial Adviser: Andrea Cascardi
Designer: Todd Ouren
Page production: Picture Window Books
The illustrations in this book were prepared digitally.

Picture Window Books
5115 Excelsior Boulevard
Suite 232
Minneapolis, MN  55416
877-845-8392
www.picturewindowbooks.com

Printed in the United States of America.

Library of Congress Cataloging-in-Publication Data
Stille, Darlene R.
I am a dolphin : the life of a bottlenose dolphin /
by Darlene R. Stille ; illustrated by Todd Ouren.
p. cm. — (I live in the ocean)
Includes bibliographical references (p.     ).
ISBN 1-4048-0596-6 (reinforced lib. bdg.)
1. Bottlenose dolphin—Juvenile literature.  I. Ouren, Todd, ill.
II. Title.

QL737.C432S74 2004
599.53'3—dc22                          2004000887

Watch me leap out of the ocean. Watch me dive down through the waves. I am a dolphin.

Scientists call me a bottlenose dolphin. Look at my curved mouth. Don't I look happy ?

A bottlenose dolphin's beak is shaped like an old-fashioned bottle. That's how the animal got its name.

3

I love to play with my friends. We play catch with big clumps of seaweed. We chase each other through the ocean waves.

Bottlenose dolphins usually live in groups of about 12. Out in the deep ocean, several hundred dolphins may live together.

4

My friends and I move together like dancers.
We leap out of the water. Then we dive down.
Look at how good we are!

A lot of people are curious about dolphins.
They take boat rides to come watch us play.
I love to surf the waves the boats make!

I'm curious about people, too. I pop up out of the
water to get a better look at them.

Since long ago, sailors have thought that seeing dolphins near their boats was good luck. The dolphins were a sign of calm weather and smooth sailing.

People say I'm one of the smartest creatures around. For me, learning tricks is a snap.

Unlike most animals, dolphins can follow commands. A dolphin can even learn a new trick just by watching another dolphin.

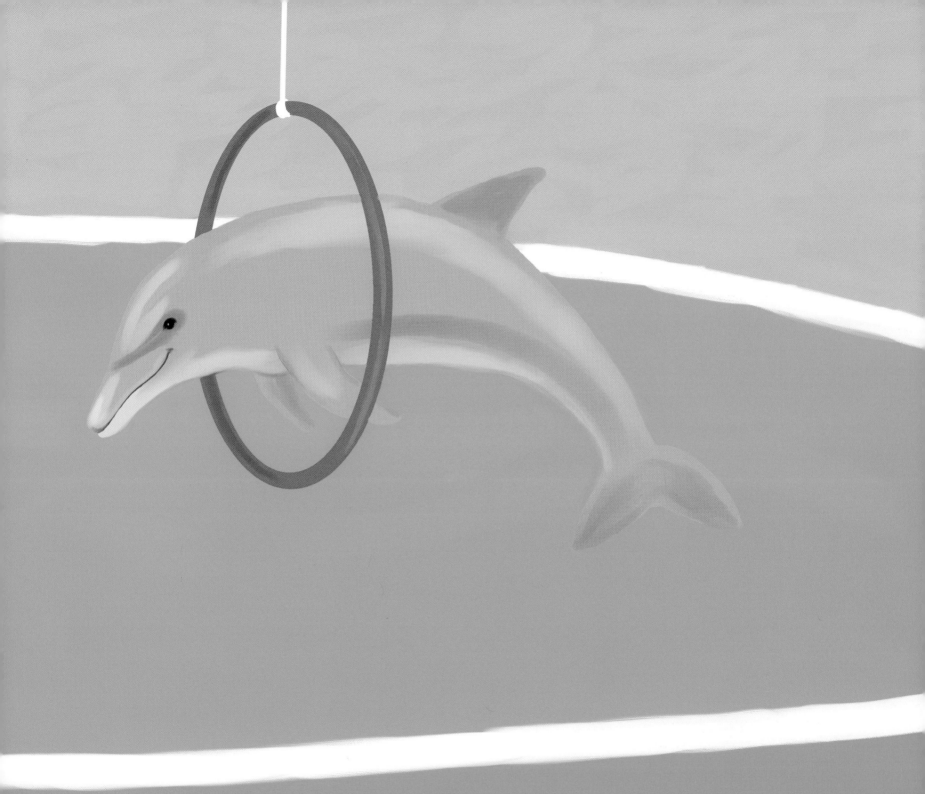

A lot of my friends perform in shows at zoos and aquariums. Have you seen them?

I'm happy with my home off the coast of Florida. The warm water feels so good against my rubbery skin.

Up, down, up, down. I pump the powerful flukes of my tail to push my body through the water. *Swoosh.*

I use my two front flippers to turn and stop.

Dolphins can swim very fast for a short way. A bottlenose dolphin can swim 23 miles (37 kilometers) per hour, about as fast as a car on a city street.

I don't stay under water for long, though. I come up every few minutes to take a big breath.

Look closely at my beak. What's missing? I don't have nostrils there. People call me a bottlenose dolphin, but I don't have a nose! I breathe through the blowhole on the top of my head.

When a dolphin sleeps, only the area around its blowhole sticks out of the water. Also, only half of a dolphin's brain sleeps at a time. The other half stays awake, so the dolphin can watch for danger.

My blowhole is just one sign that I'm a mammal. Another sign is that my mother took care of me when I was a calf.

Dolphins are affectionate. Mothers and calves rub their bodies against one another. Dolphins' skin is very sensitive to touch.

For five years, I stayed with my mother. We usually traveled with other moms and their babies.

Now I hang out with a bunch
of my friends.
**Screee.** Slap. **Smack!**
We make a lot of noises. That's how
we talk to one another.

A dolphin makes a special
sound if it needs help. Other
dolphins rush to it. Using
their backs and flippers,
they hold the injured dolphin's
head out of the water so
it can breathe.

Each one of us makes our own sound.
None of our voices sound exactly alike.

I also use my voice to find food. That must seem pretty weird to you!

When I'm hunting in dark or murky water, I make special clicking sounds. The sounds make echoes when they bounce off fish. I can tell where the fish are by how the echo sounds when it comes back to me.

A dolphin has tiny ear holes on the sides of its head, but the animal hears mostly through its lower jaw.

19

*Snap!* I grab the fish with my sharp teeth. I fill up my belly. Then it's time to play again.

Bottlenose dolphins know where to find easy meals. The dolphins recognize fishing boats. Sometimes a dolphin swims behind a boat. It snatches up the fish that fishermen throw back in the sea.

I have the greatest life! It's no wonder I always seem to have a smile on my face.

# Look Closely at a Bottlenose Dolphin

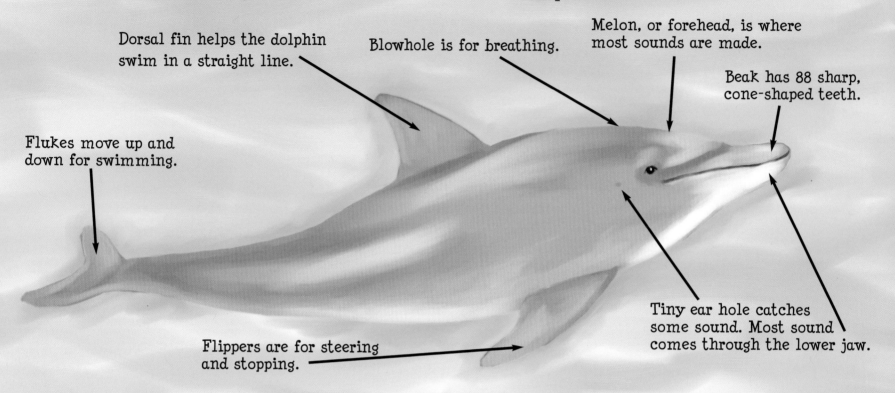

Dorsal fin helps the dolphin swim in a straight line.

Blowhole is for breathing.

Melon, or forehead, is where most sounds are made.

Beak has 88 sharp, cone-shaped teeth.

Flukes move up and down for swimming.

Tiny ear hole catches some sound. Most sound comes through the lower jaw.

Flippers are for steering and stopping.

# Fun Facts

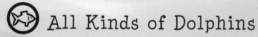 **All Kinds of Dolphins**
There are 34 kinds of dolphins that live in the sea. Most of them are black, brown, or gray. Some dolphins have light stripes or patterns.

**All Kinds of Homes**
Dolphins live in nearly all the world's oceans. Hourglass dolphins live in icy water near Antarctica. River dolphins live in freshwater rivers.

**Hush!**
Loud noises from ships and underwater equipment can make some areas of the ocean quite noisy. Scientists worry that the noises drown out dolphins' calls to one another. The noises could also interfere with the dolphins' ability to find food through echoes.

###  We Go Way Back

Dolphins have had a special relationship with people for thousands of years. Some ancient people thought dolphins were like angels. In ancient Greece, killing a dolphin was considered as bad as killing a person.

###  Stinky Fish? No Problem!

Dolphins have excellent sight and hearing. They are very sensitive to touch and can taste a little, but they have no sense of smell.

###  A Better Look

Dolphins can see well from side to side, but they can't see up. That's why a dolphin might swim on its back to chase a fish. When swimming by a ship, a dolphin might turn on its side to get a good look at the people looking down at it.

###  Better Than Birthday Candles

A dolphin's teeth grow in layers like rings around a tree. Scientists can tell how old a dolphin is by counting the number of layers that form its teeth. In the wild, dolphins live about 17 years. They can live for up to 50 years, though!

# Glossary

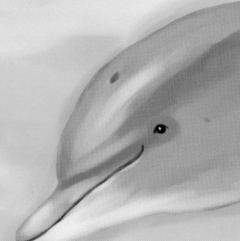

aquarium—a place where people keep fish and other water animals

blowhole—the hole on top of a dolphin's head that it uses for breathing

calf—a baby dolphin

flippers—a dolphin's two front limbs that look like paddles

flukes—a dolphin's flat tail fins

mammal—a warm-blooded animal that drank its mother's milk when it was a baby; a mammal cannot breathe under water

# To Learn More

## At the Library

Pfeffer, Wendy. *Dolphin Talk: Whistles, Clicks, and Clapping Jaws.* New York: HarperCollins, 2003.

Richardson, Adele D. *Dolphins: Fins, Flippers, and Flukes.* Mankato, Minn.: Bridgestone Books, 2001.

Waxman, Laura Hamilton. *Diving Dolphins.* Minneapolis: Lerner Publications, 2003.

## On the Web

FactHound offers a safe, fun way to find Web sites related to this book. All of the sites on FactHound have been researched by our staff.

1. Go to www.facthound.com
2. Type in this special code: 1404805966
3. Click the FETCH IT button.

Your trusty FactHound will fetch the best sites for you!

# Index

## Look for all the books in this series:

I Am a Dolphin
The Life of a Bottlenose Dolphin

I Am a Sea Turtle
The Life of a Green Sea Turtle

I Am a Shark
The Life of a Hammerhead Shark

I Am a Fish
The Life of a Clown Fish

I Am a Seal
The Life of an Elephant Seal

I Am a Whale
The Life of a Humpback Whale